Kayaking out on the water is peaceful and a fun activity for anyone. Great book for kids.

Kayaking
DAY

I0178109

Set 11 - Book 3

Berkeley
Boys
Books

Caleb Berkeley
(Bestselling Author,
Creator of over 90 books)

Elisha Berkeley
(Creator of over 70 books)

Kayaking Day (Berkeley Boys Books)

By: Caleb and Elisha Berkeley

Print ISBN: 978-1-77850-002-2

Published by C.M. Berkeley Media Group

www.cmberkeleymediagroup.com

Other Great Books

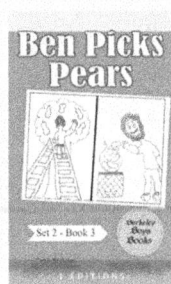

Time to Paint! — Set 5 · Book 2 — Berkeley Boys Books — EDITIONS

Trip to the Library — Set 5 · Book 3 — Berkeley Boys Books — EDITIONS

Playing Catch is FUN — Set 5 · Book 1 — Berkeley Boys Books — EDITIONS

Walk the Dog — Set 4 · Book 5 — Berkeley Boys Books — EDITIONS

Snow Day — Set 4 · Book 4 — Berkeley Boys Books — EDITIONS

Ride the Bike — Set 4 · Book 3 — Berkeley Boys Books — EDITIONS

Jason Goes Fishing — Set 4 · Book 2 — Berkeley Boys Books — EDITIONS

Cam Does His Chores — Set 4 · Book 1 — Berkeley Boys Books — EDITIONS

Dane Flies the Plane — Set 3 · Book 5 — Berkeley Boys Books — EDITIONS

Kick the ball — Set 3 · Book 2 — Berkeley Boys Books — EDITIONS

Jack Splits Wood — Set 3 · Book 1 — Berkeley Boys Books — EDITIONS

It's Picnic Day — Set 3 · Book 4 — Berkeley Boys Books — EDITIONS

Johnnie uses his Drone — Set 3 · Book 3 — Berkeley Boys Books — EDITIONS

Build a Shed — Set 2 · Book 5 — Berkeley Boys Books — EDITIONS

Ace Grows Potatoes — Set 2 · Book 4 — Berkeley Boys Books — EDITIONS

Ben Picks Pears — Set 2 · Book 3 — Berkeley Boys Books — EDITIONS

Grab these titles at Amazon, Barnes and Noble and other major online book sellers.

Caleb and Elisha Berkeley

Other Great Books

Grab these titles at Amazon, Barnes and Noble and other major online book sellers.

Other Great Books

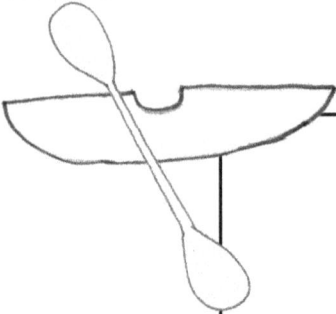

Place your
photo here.

Name:

_____

Age:

_____

City:

_____

This is Ryan

I love kayaking

Ryan
loves
kayaking

He has a kayak

He has a paddle

Ryan goes to the lake

Ryan sees Noah

I like kayaking

Noah loves kayaking

Ryan gets in his kayak

Noah gets in his kayak

They both kayak

They both had fun

The End

New words we learned today!

1. Kayak
2. Paddle
3. Like
4. Lake
5. Goes
6. See

7. Both
8. Fun
9. Loves
10. Has
11. Kayaking
12. Gets

It's time for a MAZE!!

Caleb and Elisha Berkeley

Word Scrambles

GYANKIKA _ _ _ _ _ _ _ _

YAKAK _ _ _ _ _

ADEPDL _ _ _ _ _ _

KLEA _ _ _ _

SOGE _ _ _ _

ESE _ _ _

HTBO _ _ _ _

NFU _ _ _

VSELO _ _ _ _ _

TSEG _ _ _ _

EIKL _ _ _ _

SHA _ _ _

Word Searches

S	T	H	U	L	S	R	S	L	Y	Y	A	T	X	A
Z	E	U	A	Q	M	Q	L	T	L	F	Z	T	Q	W
T	U	Y	I	S	Q	E	Y	C	J	A	Q	L	Y	Q
M	W	F	Q	H	Y	G	Q	W	B	U	A	W	N	P
I	D	A	P	Z	S	N	I	T	N	K	Y	Y	B	U
V	E	E	C	D	K	I	U	O	E	X	G	D	P	U
E	G	K	K	S	V	K	N	W	W	M	O	B	L	B
P	U	P	A	I	M	A	D	E	I	E	E	S	F	A
I	B	M	A	Y	L	Y	Q	Y	A	B	S	C	X	L
I	H	V	Q	D	A	A	J	A	Q	F	O	F	O	J
E	Y	G	I	V	D	K	M	C	L	L	U	T	A	Z
P	B	V	Y	V	S	L	H	T	F	O	I	N	H	M
D	V	P	S	B	W	T	E	F	C	V	A	E	E	I
H	A	U	Y	G	Y	K	E	G	Q	E	H	E	E	J
F	S	W	L	E	P	O	M	G	P	S	E	S	G	C

BOTH	KAYAK	PADDLE
FUN	KAYAKING	SEE
GETS	LAKE	
GOES	LIKE	
HAS	LOVES	

Caleb and Elisha Berkeley

About Caleb Berkeley

Caleb Berkeley is a published author since he was 7 years old. He is a product of the Montessori school. At 16, he's a veteran storyteller and creator of the popular children's book series, The Adventures of Moshe Monkey and Elias Froggy. Caleb is the creator of over 50 books with more coming soon. Caleb created puzzle books, easy reader books, planners, journals, writing books, and learning books for kids. Caleb is also a videographer, and video editor and the co-founder of the BerkeleyChefs channel. The BerkeleyChefs channel is a plant-based channel that was created to help parents and kids have fun cooking healthy meals together. You can check the channel on: berkeleychefs.com. Caleb is also a game card creator and an accomplished self-taught painter whose artwork has been featured at a local art gallery and the Whitby Public Library. He has sold a few of his original pieces and you can buy prints or originals for your family at: berkeleyfamilyart.com. Caleb likes to learn new stuff and do gardening in his spare time.

About Elisha Berkeley

Elisha Berkeley is an author following his brother. His first book was published at the age of 7. At the age of 12, Elisha's been working hard to create helpful books for kids. Elisha is currently an author of over 30 books. Elisha created easy reader books, a planner, writing books, and learning books for kids. Elisha is also the co-founder of the BerkeleyChefs channel along with his brother Caleb. You can check the channel on: berkeleychefs.com. Elisha is also an accomplished self- taught painter whose artwork was also featured in a local art gallery and in the Whitby Public Library. His original art pieces as well as prints are available for your family to enjoy. He has sold a few of his original pieces and you can buy prints or originals for your family at: berkeleyfamilyart.com. In his spare time, Elisha likes to make smackalicious foods, and spend time outdoors.

Answers to the Puzzles

GYANKIKA = KAYAKING

YAKAK = KAYAK

ADEPDL = PADDLE

KLEA = LAKE

SOGE = GOES

ESE = SEE

HTBO = BOTH

NFU = FUN

VSELO = LOVES

TSEG = GETS

EIKL = LIKE

SHA = HAS

Grab set 5 today at major online bookstores

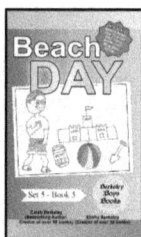

More from CM Berkeley Media Group

CM Berkeley Media Group, based in Canada, works with its authors to produce books which help to uplift the human spirit, spread the message of health and wellness, and offer practical insights in finances, and other areas.

Website: cmberkeleymediagroup.com

Grab these other great titles at Amazon worldwide and other major online booksellers.

For Adults

- Break The Poverty Curse: Unlock Your Prosperity 2022 & 2023 Success Planner - School of Prophets Edition
  (A Great tool for 17 to 70. This contains more information to help structure your life spiritually and in this life.
- Break The Poverty Curse: Unlock Your Prosperity (2017 Edition)
- Break The Poverty Curse: Unlock Your Prosperity 2019 Success Planner
  (A Great tool for 10 to adults. Learn basic necessary life planning skills)
- Break The Poverty Curse: Unlock Your Prosperity 2019 Success Planner - ULTIMATE Edition
  (A Great tool for 17 to adults. This contains more information to help structure your progress)
- Break The Poverty Curse: Unlock Your Prosperity 2019 Success Planner - WRITER'S Edition
  (A great tool for 17 to adults who have dreams of becoming an author. Use this planner to write your book in under a year)
- Break The Poverty Curse: Unlock Your Prosperity - Puzzle Power 1
- Break The Poverty Curse: Unlock Your Prosperity - Puzzle Power 2
- Break The Poverty Curse: Unlock Your Prosperity - Puzzle Power 3

- Break The Poverty Curse: Unlock Your Prosperity - CRASH PROOF (coming soon)

Caleb and Elisha Berkeley

Jenny's 99 Health Quotes To Empower Your Life

Eating4Eternity: Unlock Your Holistic Health Lifestyle. Sweet Raw Desserts: Life Is Sweet Raw™

Can I Offer You A Cigarette: The Only Sure Way To Break The Smoking Habit

Colon By Design: Overcoming The Stigma Of Colon Sickness And Unlocking True Colon Health™

Fresh Food4Life™: The Case For Taking Back Control of Your Food And Empowering Your Family And Community.

For Teens and Young Adults

The Youth Leadership Empowerment System™

Jump into the world of Dr Vicktor Maximitas, world famous psychologist by day and legendary demon hunter by night. Go into this mystery world where good triumphs over evil and souls are rescued from demonic clutches. This is a new series by Vaughn Berkeley.

- A Maximitas Novel: Unholy Fyre (Book 1)
- A Maximitas Novel: Unholy Fyre (Book 2)
- A Maximitas Novel: Unholy Fyre (Book 3)

For Children

The Adventures of Moshe Monkey and Elias Froggy book series.

- The Adventures of Moshe Monkey and Elias Froggy: A Healthy Business (Volume 1)
- Moshe and Elias Build A Garden (The Adventures of Moshe Monkey and Elias Froggy) (Volume 2)
- Moshe and Elias Tropical Vacation (The Adventures of Moshe Monkey and Elias Froggy) (Volume 3)
- Living Foods for Boys and Girls (The Adventures of Moshe Monkey and Elias Froggy) (Volume 4)
- Moshe Monkey Breaks His Leg (The Adventures of Moshe Monkey and Elias Froggy) (Volume 5)
- Moshe And Elias 2019 Daily Success Planner
- Moshe Monkey And Elias Froggy 2019-2020 Back to

Kayaking Day (Berkeley Boys Books)

School Success Planner

- Moshe Monkey And Elias Froggy: Puzzle Book (1 to 9)
- Fun with your ABC's
- The Amazing Colouring and Learning Book of Fruits and Veggies
- 2020 Biblical Planner
- School of the Prophets for Children Planner - Ultimate Edition
- Moshe Monkey And Elias Froggy - Daily Journal
- Baldy's Life
- Baldy's Writing Book for New Words
- Berkeley Short Stories, Doodles and Writing Prompts
- Scripture Brain Power 1
- Scripture Brain Power 2
- Roll the Ball
- Mom and Dad
- Ann Can Count To 10
- My Easy Cursive Handwriting Book
- Bounce the Ball
- Mow the Lawn
- Mouzzie Goes Home (Mouzzie Mouse Adventures) (Book 1)

Plus there are many more books to entertain new readers while teaching them about important life lessons.

* * * * *

Check out these titles on Amazon and major online book sellers.

Great Resources

Berkeley Chefs (berkeleychefs.com)
The Berkeley Chefs channel is where parents can find videos and recipes on how to cook healthy, delicious, plant-based meals with there kids.

Berkeley Family Art (berkeleyfamilyart.com)
This site showcases the original artwork by members of the Berkeley Family. You can order originals and prints from this site.

VaughnBerkeley.com
Vaughn's site for those on a spiritual journey to get closer to our God and creator.

CM Berkeley Media Group (cmberkeleymediagroup.com)
CM Berkeley Media Group is the digital media company founded by Vaughn Berkeley. The company publishes books that have a message to uplift individuals. There are books for children, teens, and adults.

The Book on Quantum Website
www.thebookonquantum.com
This is the website to find all the information on current books and upcoming books in the series, "The Book on Quantum", by Vaughn Berkeley.

EternityWatch Magazine
(www.eternitywatchmagazine.com)
Great site for vegan, raw-vegan, and holistic health and wellness information.

Eating4Eternity.org (www.eating4eternity.org)
Eating4Eternity is founded by Jenny Berkeley and is focused on her personal coaching approach. On the site, you will find news articles on health and wellness.

Berkeley Academy (http://berkeley.academy)
This is the online educational institute founded by Vaughn Berkeley and carrying on the tradition and heritage of the Berkeley name and role in educating the masses. Vaughn's passion has been education from as long as he can remember.

www.ingramcontent.com/pod-product-compliance
Lightning Source LLC
Chambersburg PA
CBHW070804050426
42452CB00012B/2485